# Lighting Candles

A 31
Day Devotional
to Inspire a Closer
Relationship
With God

Terrie Sizemore

This is a work of non-fiction.

Text and illustrations are copyrighted by

T Lee Sizemore, DVM, RN ©2018

Library of Congress Control Number: 2018907519

All rights reserved.

No part of this book may be

reproduced, transmitted, or stored in an information retrieval

system in any form or by any means,

graphic, electronic, or mechanical without prior written

permission from the author.

First Edition 2018

Printed in the United States of America

A 2 Z Press LLC

PO Box 582

Deleon Springs, FL 32130

bestlittleonlinebookstore.com

bestlittleonlinebookstore@gmail.com

386-681-7402

ISBN: 978-1-946908-89-6

# Dedication

**This book is dedicated to her father,
Edwin Sizemore.
I thank him for believing for and
praying for me to have faith.**

# Day 1- Exhilarate

Exhilarate - means to enliven, invigorate, stimulate, make merry or cheerful. I wonder what it's like to ride along the wild currents of a river filled with twists and turns and ups and downs that would, truthfully, take my breath away- for real - and I would die. I think of extreme sports like bungee jumping, sky diving, or hang gliding that I am also convinced I would die doing. I watch the Olympics and see downhill skiing, figure skating, cross country horseback riding, etc. Such thrilling activities that would be 'exhilarating.' In the end, all I do includes sledding on small hills in the neighborhood in the winter time. Pathetic really.

When I was a young girl, I read books about horses - the Black Stallion series by Walter Farley were my favorite. I am sure reading books allows most of us to enjoy experiences we will never actually participate in. As for the horses, I actually did ride and jump and race across fields at full speed on those gorgeous creatures I have always loved. I can say there is nothing like the real thing. Do not get me wrong, reading is and has been lovely, but really riding has made my life terrific.

My favorite author is CS Lewis. In the movie made of him and his soon-to-be wife, Joy Gresham, there were conversations about real experience v. reading about experiences. She felt personal experience trumped reading. He asked her if reading was a waste? She thought about it and said, "No," however, she still felt if one had to choose, real experience was more valuable than just reading about experiences of others.

That being said, I know I will never run an army mission into enemy territory, so reading someone's account of their experience helps me enjoy the memory and times experienced. I also do not think I will visit Paris or Vienna, but enjoy reading about them and dreaming of maybe visiting one day. So, I like to do things, but also like to read about things I find interesting.

I feel that friendship is something enjoyed more in real experience than to read about famous friendships like Gayle Sayers and Brian Piccolo. Their stories inspire me to be a better friend, but I treasure the friends and relationships I enjoy. I have the greatest friends and family that have been there for the good days and the difficult days, celebrated the wins and cried with me in the losses. They talk when I need someone to listen and I find it is wonderful to be a friend to them also. I can talk about my friends all day long, but until you meet them, they will still be strangers to you.

The Bible talks about real experience as well. In 1 John 1:1-2, it tells us'.... (the followers of Jesus) are writing about the Word of Life - in Him Who existed from the beginning, Whom we have heard, Whom we have seen with our own eyes, Whom we have gazed upon for ourselves and have touched with our own hands. And the Life - an aspect of His being- was revealed (made manifest, demonstrated), and we saw [as eyewitnesses] and are testifying to and declare to you the Life, the eternal Life in Him Who already existed with the Father and Who [actually] was made visible (was revealed) to us - His followers....'

The most exhilarating experience I have ever had is knowing the Living God. I can share experiences over and over and, the truth is, He wants all of us to have personal experience with how exhilarating He is. He is real, He is waiting, and He wants to show each of us how Great and Wonderful He truly is.

Write how you came to know Jesus. Are you finding it 'exhilarating?' Describe your experience.

_____
_____
_____
_____
_____
_____
_____
_____
_____
_____

# Day 2 - Perseverance

Prayer equals love in my opinion. There is a debate among people of faith. Some feel if a prayer is prayed, the work is done. They claim that faith says 'the thing asked for was presented to God, so there is no need to continue to make petition.' Others feel persevering prayer is necessary at times. I have been on both sides of this debate at different times in different circumstances.

I believe prayer is the mystery of Christianity and prayers are not only powerful, they are precious - Revelation 5.8 tells us "...and they had golden bowls full of incense (fragrant spices...), which are the prayers of God's people (the saints)." God saves our prayers.

At times, I am deceived to feel my prayers do not matter. Sometimes delays in answers cause this. Sometimes others' opinion that God does whatever He wishes without regard for our prayers causes my deception. Many challenge the worth of prayer by pointing out how some prayers *never* get answered. I choose to pray anyway in faith that prayer impacts the unseen world. I do not know what happens as I pray, but God does.

The Bible gives me several examples of persevering prayer. One personal favorite is in 1 Kings 18.41-45. There has been no rain for an extended time. Elijah begins to pray for rain, but nothing happens. He servant even says, "There is nothing." But Elijah continues to pray. In fact, he prayed 7 times. Then, finally, a small cloud began to form. As they continued to watch, bigger and bigger and more and more clouds formed until it began to pour. Answered prayer.

In the Book of Esther, the people were in danger. The Bible says she began to "...make supplication ...and plead ...for the lives of her people." (Esther 4.8) I have loved ones with difficulties that are of great concern to me. I am convinced my love for these individuals is pale in comparison to the love God has for them. As I read scripture, I see how Esther was moved to help her 'people.'

I also read how healing happened when fathers and mothers asked for their children, such as in Matthew 8.5-13. This compels me to be bold in prayer and hold nothing back. I pray that the ones I love have healthy relationships, be happy in life, be well, have healed hearts and bodies and minds, have good lives, strong positive behavior patterns and leave the old destructive lives behind. I pray because my

Savior died and is alive for all these prayers to be answered.

I pray without ceasing. (1 Thessalonians 5.17)

Write how you feel about prayer. Who is on your list of prayer concerns? Are you developing a prayer life?

# Day 3 - Something Old, Something New

My Aunt asked me once why I read the same Book over and over. She said she thought it would be boring. I said that I have read the Bible over and over for over 40 years because each and every day, the Living God shows me something new in His Word. It is the most exciting thing that happens to me. When I sit to read, I open my Bible and ask, 'What will the Lord say to me today?'

I am never disappointed. The Word comes alive as I read it over and over. The Lord is faithful each time I need a Word from Him to show me a special Word for the moment I need it. Recently, I have been consumed with care for my loved ones. Sometimes I think God has forgotten us, but I am very wrong. He is on the job at all times, in all places, and for all things that concern me and my loved ones.

During Bible study one night, I experienced something that is old as something new to me. The Book of Exodus was written many years ago and I read this Book many times during the over 40 years I have spent reading my Bible. Somehow, I had never seen Exodus 28 in any particular way. In fact, the verses had no significant meaning to me until a few days ago. The verses read: "and you will take two onyx stones and engrave the names of the sons of Israel..." I sensed God whispering something new to me as He said, "and you will take two onyx stones and engrave the names of your loved ones.." The Word continues, "and Aaron shall bear their names before the Lord on his shoulders of remembrance..." God again whispered to me, "and you shall bear your loved ones' names before the Lord on your shoulders of remembrance." The Word continues, "there shall be .... stones with the names of..... and they shall be on Aaron's heart, when he goes in before the Lord..." God again whispered to me, "Your loved ones shall be on your heart when you come to Me." And they are.

The ones I love truly are on my heart and I come before the Lord for them. The ones of my family, the ones I meet each and every day, the ones I know struggle. The poor and homeless I see. The ones that the Living God has not forgotten. They are on my heart as living stones that have their names engraved upon my heart as symbolism as I go before the Living God in prayer for them.

He has not forgotten us and reminds me in a special and personal way through His Word each and every time I open my beloved Bible to see what He will say to me today. What will He use to encourage me today? What will He use to teach me today? What will He use to guide me today? It's all there, waiting for me to open the Bible and spend time with Him and His Word. He shows me He is waiting for me to bring the loved ones on my heart to Him in prayer. Who's on your heart to take to the Lord today?

Write how you make time each day for Bible reading and how you find God in that time.

# Day 4 - Pearls and Paradox

Pearls are one of my favorite gems. They are pretty, elegant, and feminine. I have several in the form of earrings and necklaces. Some white, some pink. I also love my Pearl of Great Price. The Bible talks about" the kingdom of heaven (being) like a man who is a dealer in search of fine *and* precious pearls, who, on finding a single pearl of great price, went and sold all he had and bought it." (Matthew 13.45-46.) God is the Pearl in this story and, I too, would let go of everything I own if needed to know and obey God.

I am convinced that people who do not know God, or about God in a personal way, have the conception that God is a 'kill-joy' and means only to take away from them to make them something they do not want to be at all. In fact, sometimes, I think people see God as hating what they are and wanting them to be something completely different. I don't think so and I think God made each of us special and loves us more than we can comprehend. He only hates the things that hurt us. The real you is what He wants you to be and we can only be that when we experience the paradox of losing ourselves to Him to find our true selves. At times I did not see the 'broken' me as something that needed fixed or healed by God.

CS Lewis also helped me sort out the dilemma as to if God really liked the real 'me' at all. In his cleverly written 'Screwtape Letters,' he writes as though the powers of darkness are training other demons to plot against God's people and triumph over them. One quote from the book was particularly interesting and true is:

(One demon, Wormwood is being instructed by another demon, Screwtape. Wormwood is told) "Wormwood, I know that the Enemy (as he refers to Jesus) also wants to detach men from themselves, but in different way. Remember, He really likes the little vermin (God's people), and sets an absurd value on the distinctiveness of every one of them. When He talks of their losing their selves, He means only abandoning the clamor of self-will; once they have done that, He really gives them back all their personality and boasts that when they are wholly His, they are more themselves than ever. The deepest likings and impulses of any man are the raw material, the starting point, with which the Enemy (Jesus) has furnished {God's people}."

When we lose our lives, we find our lives in God. All of God's Word demonstrates how much He loves us and cherishes us as the creation He made. After all, He came to Earth to die so we could live. When we choose His way - we live and thrive, when we choose against His way, we choose death. The choice is always ours to make. I choose life.

Write how you feel you are surrendering to Jesus and finding your life as you lose it in Him.

_____
_____
_____
_____
_____
_____
_____
_____
_____
_____
_____
_____
_____
_____
_____
_____
_____
_____
_____
_____
_____
_____
_____
_____

# Day 5 - Real

Many, many years ago, (sad to admit this) there was a television show called, "To Tell the Truth." There were three contestants - one was the 'real' person the other two pretended to be the 'real' person. The players asked questions to determine who was 'real' person and who was pretending. The identity of the 'real' person was hidden until the players guessed who they felt the 'real' person was of the three. After the votes were in, the host of the show would say, 'will the real .... please stand up.' Then the real party would stand.

Sometimes I ask, "Will the REAL God please stand up." At times in life, I have had an incorrect image of God.

Often, I asked myself, 'Who is this King of Glory?'
Is He a harsh taskmaster - like Pharaoh -
telling me to make bricks, make more bricks, make bricks without straw?
Is He a frightening being - just waiting to send fire and brimstone down to Earth and on me for making the same mistake over and over?

Is He a loving God - Who is always there waiting to show me new ways He has to comfort and take care of me and love me unconditionally?
Is He dependable?
Trustworthy?
Is He the God Who can do anything and wants to do everything for me?

Who is He to you and me? Big question.

When I was a little girl, my mom took me to church. The church was big and everyone sang to organ music. I remember sitting in the pew looking up at the high ceilings, stained glass windows, and all the pictures and statues in the church. The whole atmosphere made me think God was big and stern and distant and unconcerned. He did not seem like the kind of Being I could tell all my inner thoughts and needs to. He was Someone I didn't think I would like to get to know. Sadly, this is how I viewed Him.

I was told that sometimes we do not see God as "He" is, we see Him as "we" are. I saw Him from a broken heart. Now I see Him much differently, I think I see Him more like He is - faithful, loving, dependable, just, and Holy. I am thankful for the change in seeing Him a little more clearly. I strive to know the 'real' Him better each day.

Our perception of God is important because it determines how we approach Him. If He is "Abba (Daddy) Father," then we approach Him as a small child approaches a kind and gentle father by crawling into his lap and expecting to be held and protected. If He is a harsh God, then it is difficult, if not impossible, for us to approach the Throne of Grace to find mercy and help in time of need. (Hebrews 4.16) If we find Him undependable, then we continue to trust in ourselves and our own abilities to figure out situations in life.

Who is He to you? Why is He 'this' to you? Do you want Him to be more and in what way?

# Day 6 - Miracles

There are over 300 different hummingbirds, over 2,000 different starfish in the ocean, over 300 different turtles, and many other different types of animals and fish and birds. Interesting and awesome as that is, there is only one *you* - ONE unique and wonderful *you*.

And God knows everything about you. He counts the number of hairs on your head (Luke 12.7), each day He thinks of you more times than sand particles on the beach (Psalm 139.18), died for you so you could be with Him in heaven (John 3.16), and is your Guide (Psalm 48.14), Teacher (Isaiah 30.20), and Healer (Exodus 15.26). Our Healer. Not only do some struggle with physical disorders, many struggle with deep hurts that cause sadness, addictions, compulsions, and more difficulties. God understands how this affects us because He said, "A merry heart is like good medicine, but a wounded spirit, who can bear that?" (Proverbs 17.22)

I have met many people who I know were hurt very deeply in life. I have been puzzled for years wondering why they do not ask God to heal those hurts. I experienced very deep hurts myself and availed myself to healing. A few people have honestly shared that they worry perhaps God will not heal them. I know one in particular felt if God did not heal him, he really would be doomed. I watched him suffer with low self-esteem, fear of success, depression, and other afflictions.

I believe Jesus died for each and every hurt and struggle and suffering we experience. The Bible tells us that we have a High Priest Who is touched with the feeling of our infirmity (any weakness, pain, inability to cope, etc.) so we can boldly go to Him and find help in our time of need. (Hebrews 4.15-16) Sometimes I think we think God only heals one way. This is not true. As a matter of fact, He healed in many ways. For instance,

Sometimes He touched the person (Mark 1.41),

Sometimes the person touched Him (Mark 5.24-34),

Sometimes He just spoke the Word (Luke 7.7) and commanded healing,

Sometimes He healed on the Sabbath (Luke 13.14),

Sometimes He spit on the ground to make mud and put the mud on the blind man's eyes (John 9.6),

Sometimes He shouted with a loud voice (John 11.43) and called Lazarus from the dead,

Jesus even healed the man's ear who was coming to arrest Him and crucify Him that Peter cut off with a sword (Luke 22.51).

Our Maker knows how to heal us. He sent His Word to heal us. (Psalm 107.20) and promised beauty for ashes (Isaiah 61.3). He may choose a way to heal us that is not just like He used to heal someone else, but the end result is healing. God's Word is filled with healing and restoration and reconciliation throughout. He does not want us to be without knowledge because He tells us {His} people perish for lack of knowledge (Hosea 4.6) and He has given us His Spirit to lead us into truth (John 16.13) - the truth about what's wrong and needs the touch of the Father. He leads us to the truth that sets us free (John 8.32). It is the lies we believe that kill us - the lies that we are defective, unworthy, cannot be healed, etc. Whatever the lie is, it is not from the Father of all Truth, it is from our enemy.

If we ask Him, He will show us our broken and hurt places, touch them, allow us to forgive the ones who hurt us, and heal us. He promises. What if He doesn't? I don't know. What if He does? It is worth going to Him for help. I believe the biggest miracle God does is heal a heart. He is still in the miracle business today.

Do you need healing? Does someone you know need healing?

## Day 7 - Forgiven

# 1 Cross +
# 3 Nails =
# 4 Given

    Many times in life, I have been in a position to choose to forgive those who have hurt me in some way or hold a grudge. To be honest, sometimes I find myself wishing the 'bad' people would 'get theirs.' Always been told 'what goes around comes around.' Sometimes it surprises me how angry I am to be hurt and would be happy if 'not so nice things' happen to my offenders. After a time of self-pity, I realize that is not what is best for me and I do not want to be the type of person who wishes harm to others.

    Jesus reminds me how He leads the way for us, as always. The greatness of Easter is something that remains every day. On that day so many years ago, after they beat Him, spit on Him, pulled His beard, took His clothes off and mocked Him, shoved a crown of thorns on His head and nailed Him to a Cross- and from that Cross- where He is in agonizing pain, bleeding profusely, balancing Himself on nails He was attached to that Cross with, and dying for the sins of the world, He asks God to 'forgive His torture-ers because they did not know what we were doing,' (Luke 23.34) as they gambled to see who get His perfect seamless clothing.

I believe that many times my offenders do not know what they are doing. I am not certain, but I would hope that if they really knew the injury they were causing - whether it is physical harm, job loss, property loss, mocking, or any other hurt - they would not continue to harm me or others. Even if they do mean me harm, just as they did to Jesus, I am still instructed to forgive. Daily God forgives me - for thinking unkind things, for not having faith, for ignoring Him, for trying to find my own way out of difficulties - taking my faith in vain - for treating the Holy as mundane and ordinary - when I need to pray for the awe that God deserves each and every day, for all the times I wish bad things to happen to the ones who hurt me... and on and on the list goes. He forgives me because I have no idea what I am doing at times. He even forgives me when I *do know* I am doing something wrong.

Forgiveness never makes what happened okay. Hurts and offenses will always come. Forgiveness allows me to heal and be free of the burden and hardship grudges bring. Selfishly, forgiveness is for me. It comes when I realize all I have been forgiven and I stop 'collecting debts' from others who do me wrong and forgive them because I realize how much I am forgiven. 1 Cross + 3 nails = 4 given.

All I have to do when I feel my hurt is look to the Man Who died for that hurt and the Divine Example He showed me on that day- He forgave unspeakable offenses and really, really meant it.

He prayed for God to forgive them and me, too. He did so, not because He was told to, but because He wanted to.

Father, please help us forgive others as you have forgiven us.

Does someone need your forgiveness? Do you need to forgive someone? Write how you are forgiving all things God is bringing to your attention.

_____
_____
_____
_____
_____
_____
_____
_____
_____
_____
_____
_____
_____
_____
_____
_____
_____
_____
_____
_____
_____
_____
_____
_____

# Day 8 - Tricked

Magic tricks are something that have always fascinated me. No matter how often I say I will not be tricked today, I still am. No matter how many times I say I will pay attention and not allow myself to be distracted, I still am. I am easy to fool that's for sure. I can never figure out how the magician did the trick. I saw David Copperfield make a tiger appear. Great trick. But the *truth* is that they are not real, they truly are tricks.

As fun as magic can be, I once heard someone say that the devil's greatest trick was making people think he doesn't exist. Interesting. We seem to live in a world that wants to embrace concepts such as this and suggest there is nothing 'bad' or nothing that we should refrain from. There is no 'evil' force. The world today wants to embrace that nothing is wrongful and if someone suggests something is wrong, then they are stoned for not having 'tolerance.' However, it seems most of our movies show the universal struggle between 'good' and 'evil.' Star

Wars - for instance - has Darth Vader and the 'dark' side and the Force on the 'good' side. I see the good v. evil in most children's movies and stories as well as adult themes and 'good' wins.

I think the devil not only made many believe he doesn't exist, another deception is that he makes them believe there are no consequences to choices made today. Undoubtedly, he is a liar, a thief, an accuser, and his ways lead to certain death. He deceives by making things that are ultimately destructive to us look like 'pleasure' and that all is okay. The devil also subscribes to the thought process that obeying God is not necessary and is what losers do. We need only look at evil men - ISIS, Hitler, and many others to see the work of evil. Sometimes it is a little more subtle in our own lives. Choices that are not what God would want us make lead to the breakup of homes, addictions, abuse, treating women in disgraceful ways, and many other life sabotaging actions.

Jesus, however, is Life. In fact, He is the Way, the Truth, and the Life. (John 14.6) The exact opposite of the devil. Our Healer, Savior, Greater than any opposition. He set His rules - commandments - to protect us. I used to think the 'rules' were burdensome, but our Loving Father gave them to us because they are the ways that lead to life and prosperity and happiness. They are protective because God made us; He knows how to protect us and what ultimately hurts us. Holy isn't a word we throw around much these days, but it is a word God uses to encourage us to life. Jesus knows all the tricks of the devil and has given us every reason to follow His teaching to have real life and happiness.

I choose to not be tricked by the devil, but believe God is my God, my Helper, my Deliverer, my Guide, my Source, my Friend, my Everything. God says to us He has put before us death and life - He encourages us to choose life. (Deut. 30.19) In everything we say and do, choose life and God's way. It is the way to happiness, health, good things.

Write how you protect yourself from being 'tricked.' And how you hold to God's Words.

_____
_____
_____
_____
_____
_____
_____
_____
_____
_____
_____
_____
_____
_____
_____
_____
_____
_____
_____

# Day 9 - No Fear Here

I understand the Bible tells us not to fear 365 times. It is the most common 'command' in the Bible. Some say that it is one reminder each day of the year to 'not fear.' Why is it so hard to trust? I shouldn't have, but I chuckled as I recently reviewed a journal entry from many years ago. I think I have come a little way along this journey of faith from where I was.

My journal entry referenced one of my favorite verses - 1 John 4.18: ".... 'fear has torment.' What was it I feared?

I feared not getting better. I feared financial demise. I feared loneliness. I feared God would give up on me. I feared all the things I faced in life were too big for Him. I feared I did not have enough faith. I feared I would fail Him. I feared my fear. I feared my anger. I feared disappointing Him. I feared the future. I feared loss. I feared things I could never control. I feared. I feared. I feared-and I did have torment.

1 John 4.18 also says, 'there is no fear in love - dread does not exist, perfect love turns fear out of doors and expels every trace of terror!'

The wonderful truth is that God loves us. The bottom line was and is that all I could or can count on for sure is Jesus and His Word. If I truly believed what God's Word says, there is no reason to fear. He is perfect Love and never fails us. How do we come to realize this everlasting love? (Jeremiah 31.3)

'I keep asking that the God of our Lord Jesus Christ, the glorious Father, may give you the Spirit of wisdom and revelation, so that you may know Him better. I pray that the eyes of your heart and understanding may be enlightened in order that you may know the hope to which He has called you, the riches of His glorious inheritance in His holy people, and His incomparably great power for us who believe. That power is the same as the mighty strength He exerted when He raised Christ from the dead and seated Him at his right hand in the heavenly realms..' (Ephesians 1.17-20) I pray this because when this becomes real inside of us, we will not fear.

Just as Jesus showed His scars to His disciples in John 20.19-20, "...though the disciples were behind closed doors for fear of the Jews, Jesus came and stood among them and said, Peace to you! He showed them His hands and His side," He shows His scars to me- the price He paid for my peace, my restoration, my provision, my answers to prayers, my favor, my success, my beloved relationship with Him, my deliverance, my happiness, and more.

This poem sums it up:

> Said the Robin to the Sparrow,
> "I would really like to know
> Why these anxious human beings
> Rush about and worry so."
> Said the Sparrow to the Robin,
> "Friend, I think that it must be,
> That they have no Heavenly Father
> Such as cares for you and me."

We do have a Heavenly Father such as cares for the sparrows. 'Don't be afraid because you are move valuable than many sparrows.'

(Matthew 10.31)

Write if you have fear. What about?

_____
_____
_____
_____
_____
_____
_____
_____
_____
_____
_____
_____
_____
_____
_____
_____
_____
_____

# Day 10 - The Road

  Sometimes I am confident and know exactly where I am going in life and how I want to get there. Directions are clear and I am on my way. Sometimes, however, I feel I wander aimlessly. No matter how hard I try, I cannot make decisions or decide which road to take.

  Sometimes my preoccupation with the cares and stresses of life cause me to drift along my path and away from my close relationship to and with the God I love. Work and family and farm life and trying to rearrange my career goals distract me from Him. These times are always empty for me. I am not meant to be far from God. My very life depends on my connection with Him. When I feel distant from God, Something deep inside makes me realize He has never left me and I feel Something calling me back to Him. I make haste to again became a pilgrim on a road back to my close encounters with God. Even in the midst of confusion about life's direction at times, the one thing I am sure of is having a heart that sincerely wants to 'Go with God.'

It is my sincere desire for "(God) to imprint His laws upon my mind, even upon my inner most thoughts and understanding, and engrave them upon my heart, and (for Him to) be my God and me His child." (Hebrews 8.10). I want "it to not be necessary for others to teach me for I will know Him myself..." (Hebrews 8.11).

The children of Israel were frightened by God and did not want to hear from Him directly, but asked Moses to hear from Him and tell them what He said. (Exodus 20.19). I always wanted - and want now - to hear from Him directly. He promised to teach us, talk to us, walk with us, be with us. What a thrill! I want the complete experience.

While comparing versions of the Bible, the New International Versions tells us in Psalm 84.5 "Blessed are those whose strength is in (God), who have set their hearts on pilgrimage." My amplified Bible for this verse states, "Blessed (happy, fortunate, to be envied) is the man whose strength is in (God), in whose heart are the highways to Zion." A little note I added in the margin of my Bible reminds me, "the road to Zion is in my heart." The road to Zion- the city of our God - where we meet with the God of the Universe- is in our hearts.

While it is true, on occasion, my heart has wandered in life; His grace has always grabbed me again and again. I strive to always have my life on track with the God I love, navigating between the ditches of life with the One Who guides every step, opens every door, provides for every need, and teaches me everything. Our hearts' pilgrimage are in His hands. We are being pursued by the God Who loves us. Make the road to Zion a determined path in your life to God.

Write about your road and present journey with God. Where are you and where do you want to go?

# Day 11 - In the Blink of an Eye

We read to know we are not alone. I am convinced this is true. I know I do.

While reading another writer's posts, I stumbled upon a letter one of his readers sent him.
It went:
I got inspired to write a poem about my late big brother. He passed on Christmas of 2017.
"...My brother.
You are gone, but you are not far away.
At the end of each day,
You are my last thought.
You are on the other side of my fear,
Therefore,
I have nothing to fear..."

I appreciate the sentiment in this short, but very sweet poem. My big brother passed in June, 2017. I do not have a poem, but he shared a song with me about 'keeping him in my heart for a while." The truth is I will keep him in my heart forever. Each of us loses ones we love eventually. When we do, we want to know we are not alone and that we will get through the loss.

While reading "The Chosen" by Chaim Potok, he shares this with his son:

'Human beings do not live forever... We live less than the time it takes to blink an eye, if we measure our lives against eternity. So it may be asked what value is there to a human life. There is so much pain in the world. What does it mean to have to suffer so much if our lives are nothing more than the blink of an eye?....I learned a long time ago,...that a blink of an eye in itself is nothing. But the eye that blinks, *that* is something. A span of life is nothing. But the man who lives that span, *he* is something. He can fill that tiny span with meaning, so its quality is immeasurable though its quantity may be insignificant.....A man must fill his life with meaning, meaning is not automatically given to life. ... A life filled with meaning is worthy of rest...."

It does seem like the blink of an eye that my brothers, my grandparents, and the others that I love lived and shared time with me. It seems like a blink of an eye when I was young and sharing moments with my family and friends. Vacationing and having summers off from school. My big brother lived his life to the fullest and enjoyed the big moments in the Florida Keys and the small moments going to lunch and a movie, or eating in and watching TV together. In the blink of an eye, it is gone, but the memories remain. In the blink of an eye, I don't hear his voice any longer, but I remember it. In the blink of an eye, it will be my turn to leave this world. I want to live a life filled with meaning like my brother and other loved ones did and live life to the fullest, like they did. In the blink of an eye, I will be reunited with all the ones I love. In the meantime, I will be with the ones I love here - to the fullest.

Write how you are living life to the fullest with God. Are you missing someone? Are you taking all the opportunities presented to do God's work?

_____
_____
_____
_____
_____
_____
_____
_____
_____
_____
_____
_____
_____
_____
_____
_____
_____
_____
_____
_____

# Day 12 - Doubts

There are times I am so convinced about my faith, nothing could shake it. Then, sometimes, something comes along and the world falls apart around me. Doubts seem to happen when I least expect them.

I am in good company. John the Baptist was related to Jesus and they must have grown up together. John is the one prophesied to come before Jesus, declaring, "Prepare the way of the Lord." He baptized Jesus. I think then he was certain Jesus was the Messiah. However, John was jailed and sentenced to death. He sent his friends to ask if Jesus really was the Messiah. Many called John the Baptist a great man of God. Now, he sat in prison, probably wondering why he wasn't delivered. Wondering why he was going to die. Wondering if Jesus truly was the Messiah, why He didn't come to save him. I love Jesus' reaction- He never responded negatively to his question. He never berated his doubts. In fact, He told the men- and I think very compassionately - tell John 'this and this.' He wanted John to be assured. The answer was 'Yes, Jesus is the Messiah.'

In addition to John, the children of Israel asked "Is the Lord among us or not?" (Exodus 17.7). They experienced God's deliverance from Egypt, protection from plagues, guidance and provision along the way after deliverance, and the parting of the Red Sea. They still doubted. God still led them, protected them, provided for them, and loved them. Sometimes I have to remind myself of how God has always come through for me too.

I also relate to when Moses cried to God with doubts and frustration. Exodus 5. 22-23 tells me, "Then Moses turned again to the Lord and said, O Lord, why have You dealt evil to this people? Why did You ever send me? For since I came to Pharaoh to speak in Your name, he has done evil to this people, *neither have You delivered Your people at all.*"

Moses knew and loved God so well he came with honest frustration and doubt. God did not rebuke Moses. He was not angry. The Bible tells us, "Then the Lord said to Moses, Now you shall see what I will do .... for ... (God said) ...I am the Lord ... I have ...established My covenant and I WILL bring you out from under the burdens ... and I WILL rescue you with an outstretched arm ... I WILL take you to Me ... I WILL be to you a God: and you will know that it is I ... and I WILL bring you into the land ... I swore that I would give ...."

Sometimes we feel doubts may be met with disappointment from the Lord, but we can be encouraged that when we come with humility and honesty, God will walk with us in our doubts until our doubts are turned to faith. His love is stronger than our doubts. He is able to bear questions. He is able to understand frustrations. I have been waiting for years for miracles in the lives of the people I love. God has promised deliverance from drugs, loneliness, hopelessness, child abuse issues, and more. Sometimes I exclaim, 'He hasn't delivered them at all.' I choose to continue in faith until God utters the words - 'Now you will see what I will do.'

As I wait, I sing:

I will praise You all my life,
I will sing to You with my whole heart
I will trust in You, my Hope and my and Help
My Savior and my Faithful God
Oh Faithful God, My Faithful God
You give me life
You uphold my cause
You dry my eyes
You're always near
You're a faithful God.

Do you sometimes doubt? Can you write what about? How is God helping with these doubts?

_____
_____
_____
_____
_____
_____

# Day 13 - The Rope

My favorite author, CS Lewis, wrote in 'A Grief Observed' that "It does not matter what we believe until its truth or falsehood is a matter of life and death. It does not matter how strong the rope is until we need it to hold us." It has always mattered to me that the God I love and believe in is the Living God and the Way to Heaven and real Life and is able to help at all times and in all circumstances. We have His Word on it.

I am convinced that there are moments in everyone's life that struggles and possibly suffering become overwhelming and hanging on is what we do at these times.

The Bible tells me, "Yet amid all these things, we are more than conquerors and gain a surpassing victory through Him Who loves us." (Romans 8.37) God promises victory, but the road can be very bumpy at times – for sure.

I love Job for many reasons. It is funny to me that I have not heard many sermons taught from Job. Most talk about his sustaining faith under suffering. Some quote he was a 'righteous man.' (1.8) Some quote the profound utterances he made, such as "my Redeemer knows the way I take and when He has tried me, I shall come forth as gold." (23.10) and "though He slay me, yet will I trust Him." (13.13) And my favorite is how I am reminded 'God restored double to him after his suffering.' (42.10)

    I truly love all these references to faith under heartbreaking and profound suffering. I only wonder why many omit what I consider the 'meat' of this book.

    I see Job as a suffering and sometimes angry man. The following verses tell me this:

"my spirit is broken, my days are spent..the grave is ready for me.." 17.1
"my complaint is bitter.." 23.2
"..but my eye pours out tears to God..." 16.20
"let me alone, so I may speak: and let come on me what may" 13.13
"I am weary of life and loathe it!" 10.1-22
"why did You bring me forth out of the womb?" 10.18
"why do You hide Your face...as if I were Your enemy." 13.24
'(is it because of sin?) 13.23
"surely I wish to speak to the Almighty, and argue.. that He may explain the conflict between what I believe of Him and what I see of Him." 13.3
"Oh, that my impatience and vexation might be..weighed and all my calamity be laid up over against the other (to see if my grief is unmanly.)

For now it would be heavier than the sand of the sea..6.1-30

As I read Job, it appears to me this man is suffering to the deepest part of his being. I, like Job, aspire to say, "and He Who vouches for me is on high." (16.19) And Job also exclaimed, "Indeed, this will turn out for my deliverance." Job 13.16 (NIV)

I know heartache and suffering happens. God was Job's rope and it was a matter of life and death to him if God was able to sustain him and bring him to a better place after his heartache and suffering ended. God is our Rope. He is our Deliverer. We can trust the Man Who died for us to be with us at all times and in all circumstances.

Do you have seasons of struggle? Write about it and write if you can ever relate to Job. Do you find others struggling? Do you have hopeful words for them?

_____
_____
_____
_____
_____
_____
_____
_____
_____
_____
_____
_____

# Day 14 - Charcoal Fires

I love charcoal fires. The warmth and the crackling sounds remind me of slower times and easier days. I always enjoy sitting around the fire talking, laughing, and sometimes singing with the sounds of frogs and insects in the background. I love roasting marshmallows and cooking over the fire. Once I was camping with a friend and we made breakfast, lunch, and dinner for three days over the coal fire. Yummy. Even thinking about the times around a charcoal fire invokes all the memories and emotions associated with those times.

There are only two times in the Bible when a charcoal fire is mentioned. The first time is in the middle of the night, when Jesus was being beaten and sentenced to death, Peter warmed himself by a charcoal fire and denied Jesus three times. (John 18.18.) Jesus knew Peter would deny Him and even told him so. Peter emphatically said he would *never* deny Jesus, but he did what he never wanted to do. Standing by that fire of coals, he denied he knew Him. Perhaps he was overwhelmed with the atrocity that was happening to the Savior, but when the rooster crowed, he had denied Jesus three times. Jesus not only knew the future events in Peter's life, He knew Peter would need healing and restoration.

So, on that post resurrection morning, Jesus went to the sea where Peter and some others had gone back fishing. He built a charcoal fire on the beach and began cooking. (John 21.9) Jesus asked Peter three times if he loved Him. How the smell and warmth of those coals must have burned in his mind as he remembered those moments and the sorrow for denying the Savior. But, the Great Psychiatrist took Peter back to the painful time and memories and Peter received healing and restoration.

Jesus has walked with all of us every day of our lives. There is no event He has not witnessed or been close to us during. He knows every hurt or disappointment or painful memory that has ever happened to each of His children and He wants us to be healed. He died on a Cross and rose from the dead to heal us. The Bible tells us 'the punishment needful for us to obtain peace was put on Him.' (Isaiah 53.5) When a situation 'pushes buttons' or creates anxiety in us or causes us to have uncomfortable memories, this is a signal there is some deep hurt that needs the touch of the Savior. It is these moments Jesus takes us back to the charcoal fires in our lives to touch those painful memories and restore us to Himself.

Like Peter, life bumps us and we hurt - sometimes very deep hurts happen and many scars. Sometimes we fall. Sometimes we are not the people we wish we were. If we do not receive the touch of the Lord, these hurts may hinder us in relationships and happiness. Jesus knows.

Jesus asked Peter three times if he loved Him - I think because Peter denied Him three times. Exasperated with shame, Peter said, "Lord you know all things, You know I love You." Jesus did know Peter loved Him, He knows we love Him. He knows we make mistakes and need His love desperately. I say this too, "Lord, You know I love You." I pray for all to love Him too.

Do you have any 'charcoal fires' in your life? If you are not certain, ask God to show you.

_____
_____
_____
_____
_____
_____
_____
_____
_____
_____
_____
_____
_____
_____
_____
_____
_____
_____
_____

# Day 15 - Michael and his Limousine

This place in Vienna looks spectacular. What a view there must be off the side of this mountain ledge. This photo makes me think all the world is sunny and happy and majestic. There are so many breathtakingly beautiful places to visit or live. Many hold special places in people's hearts. I have heard of Fiji, Hong Kong, Sidney, London, Paris, the Grand Canyon, and many, many more places on Earth. Sometimes it is not even a 'wonder-of-the-world-type' place that means so much to us, sometimes it's just home with loved ones.

I think this planet is amazing. There is a place for everyone. Some like the mountains, some the ocean waters. Some like the farm life, some the big city. I have loved many places. I lived in the city when I was young and enjoyed the noise and hustle and bustle of the activities there. I also lived on a farm and when I sat on my front porch looking at my three-acre front yard and watching the cars go by, I felt only God knew I was there. My brother loved the rivers in Florida and considered the Florida Keys 'home.' As great as this Earth is, I believe heaven is lovely and great beyond imagination. My brother went to heaven. I know he dines with the King and is in Paradise. I think he has found the rivers in heaven too.

My friend Joyce has a son with cystic fibrosis. His name is Michael. Everyone prayed and prayed for Michael to be healed. Even in the midst of faith, his condition worsened. One night, in a lonely hospital room in Cleveland, Ohio, he and his mother shared his last moments. He was barely able to breath, but he sat up in bed, looked at her, and said, "Mom, Jesus is here for me in my limousine." Young Michael always wanted to ride in a limousine. Jesus knew. With tears in her eyes, her little boy looked at her and said, "You have to let me go, Mom." He was only twelve.

She knew, but it hurt. I know the ones that have gone before us are truly happy and would never want to return to this Earth, but the holes in our hearts are great and the tears we cry are real. Sometimes there is comfort in knowing they are waiting for us and one day we will all be together again. Sometimes it is comforting to know that There the streets are gold, there is no need for the light because Jesus is the Light, there are no more tears, no more struggles, no fear, no lack, and no sickness - it is Paradise.

Until the day we join those that have gone before us, we keep loving, caring, and struggling and helping each other make it through every day.

Write your thoughts about heaven.

# Day 16 – Oops!

If I had a nickel for every time I did something foolish or thoughtless or just plain 'stupid,' I'd be a very rich woman. Seems I cannot go a day without something. Most don't know because I wisely don't tell all my mishaps. In fact, I forgot some important items I meant to take to work today. No real big deal, but a real big inconvenience.

Sometimes it's easy to have a tendency to freely give unsolicited advice on just how not to make mistakes each day. How to be more organized, less forgetful - perfect really. We even hear others shouting out ways to be better at just about everything. Easier to *give* advice than *follow* that advice.

Recently, I heard a cute little story about a young girl who took her homework to church. She enjoyed the service, but after it was over, she unintentionally forgot her homework in the church. She informed her mother of her situation. As they returned to retrieve the homework, her mother proceeded to scold her the entire way back to church. She told the young girl how she needed to be more responsible and make sure she did not forget important things like her homework. The little girl quietly listened as they drove along. When they arrived back at the church, the little girl went in to find her homework. Soon, she came out of the church, walking with a happy and bouncy stride. She was smiling from ear to ear. The little girl had her homework in one hand and her mother's purse in the other.

I must admit I find that one cute little story. I was feeling sorry for the young girl being scolded for being distracted in church and making an innocent mistake. I wondered how her mom felt when she saw her purse being toted along with her daughter's homework. Very funny. It all reminds me of how easy it is for me to hold others to a standard I do not always hold myself to. I do not have any stones to throw at anyone who finds themselves in a situation where things most likely could have gone better, but didn't.

I want to take time to extend a gracious attitude to all those around me who are as imperfect as I am.

I want to be the person people think I am when there is no one watching. I want to be gracious behind the wheel and in the store and when I am around others that may not know Jesus.

How can you show patience to others – to family and friends and even strangers?

# Day 17 - Unnoticed by the World, Noticed by God

    I would guess that most of us have small lives. We muddle through life mostly unnoticed by the world, but we are noticed by God. In fact, in God's economy, the least on this Earth are the greatest in the Kingdom of God (Luke 9.48) and blessed are the poor in spirit because theirs is the Kingdom of God. (Matthew 5.3)

    This is the exact opposite message of today's world. The rich and famous make the popular list. But I know God sees us ones who feel insignificant and unnoticed - let me tell you about Louie. When I first gave my heart to Jesus, I wanted everyone to know Him. My heart was captivated by the Creator of the Universe Who came to Earth so I could know Him and have the most wonderful friendship I could have ever imagined. Jesus called me 'friend.' (John 15.15)

    I was just a young girl, but my zeal caused me to ride my bicycle seven miles from my home to a college town to share my newfound faith with several students there. I went on and on about this Jesus of mine and how wonderful He is and how He wanted their hearts too. In frustration, one man, Louie, said to me, "Where was God when I prayed to Him and I was in the gutter with no food, no home, no money, and I prayed."

To be honest, I was speechless. What do you say to someone who really wanted help from God and prayed and came to the conclusion God let him down? I went home dejected. It seemed he won. God did not come through as hoped and Louie was not about to give his heart to a God Who could not be trusted. When I began to pray that evening, I asked God, "Where were you when Louie prayed?" As I sat quietly, God spoke to my heart and said, 'I answered every one of Louie's prayers.'

Stunned, I began to realize how God had done super abundantly above and beyond all that Louie had prayed or even hoped- just as He promises in Ephesians 3.20. God showed me that Louie was in this really great private college for free - he was on a football scholarship - had a roof over his head - and food in his tummy - and was accomplishing an education to take care of things as he completed his education. All free to him. How good and faithful God is.

Now, it is true, an angel did not come down with a tray of food and word that there was money under the plate and keys to a hotel room.... But God did hear Louie and did answer. Louie missed it. I never saw Louie again to tell him what God showed me, but I have always prayed for God to show me how He answers us and how He has an endless supply.

The Earth is the Lord's and fullness thereof. Psalm 24.1. He owns all the jobs and all the cars and all the houses and all the everything. It is the Father's good pleasure to give us the Kingdom. (Luke 12.32.) He sees and hears you and your prayers for help and family and people who come into your lives in need. Continue to pray. Continue to believe. Ask for eyes to see His answers and always remember to thank Him.

Write how you want to see Jesus in the answers when your prayers are answered.

_____
_____
_____
_____
_____
_____
_____
_____
_____
_____
_____
_____
_____
_____
_____
_____
_____
_____
_____
_____
_____

# Day 18 - The Lion and the Lamb

As we look ahead each New Year in our lives, many of us, or ones we love, will face many challenges. I always look to the Bible for help.

Sometimes I think many people consider Jesus and God as weak or so meek that He is not up for today's challenges. In the Bible, Jesus is referred to as a Lion and a Lamb. Without a doubt, there is a huge contrast between the two. I must admit, my personal experience with Him has been Him as a Lamb- the Lamb of God slain for the sins of the world- but also, I have found Him a Lamb because He is always gentle and kind to me. He knows I cannot bear harshness or feelings of overwhelming condemnation for not being able to be the exact person I would like to be.

However, he has been a Lion as well. He is ferocious in wanting to protect us and our loved ones from harm and defend us in every way. I believe there is nothing He won't do for us. Some areas of scripture make me think this as well.

For instance, this is how God reacts when He hears us calling - "In my distress ... I cried to my God for help; He heard my voice from His temple, and my cry for help came before Him, into His *very* ears. Then the earth shook and quaked, the foundations of the mountains trembled; they were shaken because He was indignant *and* angry. Smoke went up from His nostrils, ... He bowed the heavens also and came down .... and He rode upon a cherub (storm) and flew; and He sped on the wings of the wind... The Lord also thundered in the heavens, and the Most High uttered His voice, hailstones and coals of fire....He reached from on high, He took me; He drew me out of many waters....." Psalm 18.6-16.

WOW- what a reaction in the heavens by God when we cry to Him for help. I pray for all of us to have eyes to see and understand how God reacts when we think our prayers are bouncing off the ceiling - eyes opened the way Elijah's servant's eyes were opened so he could see that the mountain was filled with chariots surrounding the man of God to help and protect him - more with him than were against him. 2 Kings 6.17. The same is true for each of us.

We are no strangers to need. Ones we love are struggling. Some with financial worries, job needs, family alienation, addiction, poor choices, compulsive behaviors, eating disorders, anxiety, depression, and other struggles? If we could do the work ourselves, prayer would not be necessary, but we pray because we need a miracle. And miracles happen.

I am so glad God is a Lion when it comes to coming to us and the ones we love to rescue all of us. And I am glad He is a Lamb that will be kind and gentle with us in our fragile state of human hood.

I pray for our eyes to be open to see the heart of God and how He is fighting for us and our loved ones in our struggles. I pray for us to pray. Ask and keep on asking, seek and keep on seeking, knock and keep on knocking, for the ones who ask will receive and the ones who seek will find and the ones who knock, the doors will be opened for. Matthew 7.7. God promised.

Write what you find Jesus as – the Lion or the Lamb. Describe why.

_____
_____
_____
_____
_____
_____
_____
_____
_____
_____
_____
_____
_____
_____
_____
_____
_____
_____
_____
_____

# Day 19 – When Things Don't Make Sense

I can imagine all of us have had seasons of difficulties. Actually, some more than others, it seems. Corrie Ten Boom - as above - survived a Nazi concentration camp. She and her family were tortured because they hid Jewish people in their home. She wrote a book about her experiences titled, "The Hiding Place." Because of a 'clerical mistake,' she was released. I see the hand of God in her release as she did. Women her age were not generally released. As people of faith, the times of difficulty test the genuineness of our faith and help us grow in faith. Corrie Ten Boom kept her faith amid horrific circumstance. She also shared that as she walked with the Lord, year after year, she *understood* less and less and just 'abided under the shadow of the Almighty' more and more. (Psalm 91.1)

Another woman of faith, Joni Earekson Tada, wrote a book and writes, "true wisdom-it's found not in being able to figure out why God allows tragedies to happen, it is found in trusting God when you can't figure things out. God is attracted to the weak, He is drawn to the needy, and He is near those who acknowledge their spiritual poverty. God lavishes His grace on those who consider themselves undeserving." That describes me as well as many of us.

Some days are more difficult than others, but we have hope. We have the Living God Who leads us and guides us each day. When He leads us into the 'wilderness' - so to speak - He walks with us. One of the most encouraging scriptures to me describing God's Divine providence and His making a way where there looked like there was not a visible way for help is Psalm 77.19 (the NLT) that reads, "Your road led through the sea…a pathway no one knew was there." God is leading and He gives hope to those who feel they have no hope. He has 1,000 ways to deliver us from our circumstances.

We are encouraged to come to place where we say what Habakkuk 3.17-18 says - "Though the fig tree does not blossom, and there is no fruit on the vines, though the product of the olive fails and fields yield no food, though the flock is cut off from the fold and there are no cattle in the stalls, Yet will I rejoice in the Lord…" He is a faithful God to help us.

Do you need assurance? Does someone you know need assurance facing a difficult time?

# Day 20 - A Motley Crew

I think many wonder what they can do for God? After all, we can't change people and God is the great and powerful and able One. We may feel like the small cub in the picture- essentially powerless or inadequate to be of help, but God - like the cub's mama - is always with us to help and protect. God chooses us to work with Him- imperfect or inadequate as we may be.

I find the ones Jesus chose to be a motley crew. James and John were the 'sons of thunder' -having tempers it seems (Mark 3.17), Peter denied Him (John 18.27), Paul was Saul and was a murderer (Acts 7.58), Thomas doubted (John 20.27), David had an affair and was a murderer, (2 Samuel 11), Jonah ran from God (Jonah 1.3), Gideon required a sign from God, (Judges 6.36) and on and on the list goes. I think they are included to let us know we are not alone when it comes to imperfection. (We need to keep trying though.)

I once told God I was not strong. He said He did not come for strong people. I said I was not well. He said He did not come for well people. I said I was not even good. He said the story is not about me. I smile as I write this, because the story truly *is* about Him and not me. 2 Corinthians 4.7 reminds me- 'we possess this Precious Treasure - the Good News of Jesus- in our frail selves, so that the greatness can be seen to be from God, and not ourselves.'

John 21 tells that after Jesus was crucified, buried, and rose from the dead 3 days later- just as He told His followers - His disciples went back fishing. What were they thinking? I can only assume that they felt the One they loved and followed was now dead and gone and they had no life to live but the lives they knew before. Jesus didn't hold this against them. They were His boys and He went to get them. I can see Him that day on the shore, making breakfast for them, inviting them to come-- waving them in- my mind hears Him saying, 'Come on boys, I'll explain it one more time..."

In Matthew 28.16-20, the passage tells that after Jesus rose from the dead, He and the remaining eleven disciples went to the mountain where Jesus ascended to heaven. They fell down and worshiped Him, but 'some doubted.' How could they doubt? They walked with Him for three years watching Him turn water into wine, raise the dead, heal lepers, give blind men sight, feed thousands with a few loaves, saw Him alive after He was brutally crucified, and more.

I have no stones to throw. I have walked with Him for over forty years and have seen Him do more miracles than I can say, but, I am ashamed to admit, I still doubt. He still loves me. His love never fails.

His message is the same today. He still comes for us no matter how many times we think we cannot do something or that we miss the road or we think we are forgotten or got it all wrong. We are His. He loved that motley crew so many years ago and He still loves and uses imperfect, weak, doubting, people today. He wants us to do His work. He is counting on us.

So, what can we do for God? We can give a cup of cold water in His name. (Matthew 10.42) We may not preach to millions and convert thousands, but we see people every day that need our smile, a pat on the back, a hug, listened to, time spent with, a few dollars for a meal, a ride somewhere, shopping for them. Yes, we can all give a 'cup of cold of water.' We can all do work for God every day as we help those in our lives. I may not be able to change the struggles my loved ones face, even though I desperately want them to be well, but I can help ease the suffering they feel each day and continue to love them.

Write how you feel Jesus uses you and if you feel He is able to use you. What are your gifts?

_____
_____
_____
_____
_____

# Day 21 - Lighting Candles

My sister in law once said, "We curse the darkness, but we forbid anyone to light a candle."

The darkness. I suppose that could be loneliness for some. Single motherhood for others. Divorce, death, alcohol or chemical addiction, compulsive tendencies, eating disorders, anger and unforgiveness issues, a past riddled with abuse, being an orphan, losing a child or never having a child or a spouse, and other struggles are the darkness for many. For others, the darkness is also the deep feelings of being unwanted, unloved, defective, unworthy, unlovable, lost, worthless, helpless, hopeless, never measuring up, like they don't 'fit in,' and feelings of failure- to name a few.

Mother Teresa is quoted as saying, 'Being unwanted, unloved, uncared for, forgotten by everybody, I think that is a much greater hunger, a much greater poverty than the person who has nothing to eat.' Although I think no one should go hungry, I certainly pray no one feels forgotten, unloved, or unwanted.

No, life is certainly not all butterflies and daisies for some. For some, it is a real struggle to get through each day. Where does one turn for help? Where does one turn for answers?

When I was in the darkness in life- one particular very dark place - I needed some candles to light my way out of the dark of deep despair. My story had to do with deep depression and other things. When trying to figure out why I was struggling so, I came across some helpful information I wanted to share.

First, I learned that God's Word says 'A merry heart is like good medicine, a cheerful mind works healing, but a wounded spirit, who can bear this?' Proverbs 17.22. I realized I was not meant to be wounded and that was why I was not handling it well.

God's word also tells us, 'He gives beauty for ashes, the oil of joy for morning, and the garment of praise for the spirit of heaviness.' Isaiah 61.3. I often wondered how my ashes could ever be something beautiful. This took time to sink in.

While in the pit I was in, the Light finally came. The truth was I was not defective. I was not helpless or worthless. I was not unlovable. The lies I believed were what were killing me, the 'Truth began to set me free.' John 8.32. The truth was lovely, kind, and wonderful.

How? Slowly, I began to learn. I read about how God felt about me and you. How He treasures us more than anything in this world. The Bible says, 'The Earth is the Lord's and the fullness of it,' Psalm 24.1. He showed me that even though He owns everything in this world, we are His most precious possession. More than houses, cars, boats, and everything, He considers us what He treasures and loves beyond our ability to comprehend at times.

When God opened my eyes to see how He treasured me above anything else, I felt loved. Hope filled my heart.

The Bible also tells me that God's thoughts are precious towards me and they are so vast they are more in number than the sand! Psalms 139.17-18. What an amazing thing to tell me.

There is hope for a hurting world. His Name is still Jesus.

Write how you think Jesus sees you. Do you feel valuable to Him? Do you need candles lit?

_____
_____
_____
_____
_____
_____
_____
_____
_____
_____
_____

# Day 22 - Thanksgiving

The day of thanks is every day. There is always something to be thankful for. Sometimes it's difficult to find that something, I realize. When I was struggling, my "Thankful" jar was empty. I could not find *one* thing to be thankful for. This is a shame-on-me thing because the truth was; I had many things to be thankful for.

Maybe the car doesn't work, anxiety is overwhelming, thoughts of quitting or hopelessness plague, bills are mounting, loneliness is discouraging, the kids aren't behaving, health issues are worrisome, things aren't going the way hoped, the addiction is unbearable, and more. I could name a hundred things that seemed to be going wrong.

As I prayed and kept trudging ahead, I began to make a choice to offer God a 'sacrifice of praise ' as in Psalm 27.6. I felt better when I did. I started by being thankful for living free in America, having great friends and family, God with me, and every simple thing I could think of to try to find at least ONE thing a day to be thankful for each day. Eventually, the list began to grow.

I am sorry to admit that being thankful was a sacrifice for me because my tendency is to only see the difficulties and not 'count my blessings' as often spoke about. I was a 'glass 1/2 empty' kinda girl. As I studied to help with the struggles I faced and what I share with others I know struggle, the scripture 2 Corinthians 10.4 became meaningful. This tells us- ' the weapons of our warfare... are strong and mighty...'

I find that the struggles we face are sometimes attacks by dark forces. We are in a battle whether or not we or our loved ones want to be. I wondered what 'our weapons' were. I realized one of my strongest weapons against the depression and struggles-and I know are helpful with addictions, compulsions, eating disorders- any struggle - is praise and a thankful heart. Being thankful is a form of praise.

The most difficult thing I experienced was the thought of being thankful for the struggle I faced. I never thought I could be thankful for the pain. The Bible tells me to be thankful in all things. (1 Thessalonians 5.18) Over time, I did begin to thank God for the pain I experienced and the situations I felt were bad and could never be considered good in life. Now, I am thankful to God for having sent the struggles into my life because they served as my pathway to Him. I know Him in a way I would never have known Him without them. Also, I became free of the struggle as the days continued.

George Mueller refers to Ro. 8.28 when he reminds us, 'In 1,000 trials, it is not 500 of them that work for the believer's good, but 999 and one beside.' All things in our life work together for good. Even the broken things and pain and discouragement and struggle I faced and we all face.

I pray for any struggling person-no matter the struggle, to find something to be thankful for and to have eyes to see that the struggle they are in can be their pathway to the Living God and become good for them and others they will eventually help in life.

Write how you want to make Thanksgiving something to do every day.

_____
_____
_____
_____
_____
_____
_____
_____
_____
_____
_____
_____
_____
_____
_____
_____
_____
_____
_____
_____
_____

# Day 23 - Am I My Brother's Keeper?

Am I my brother's keeper? This question intrigues me. In the society I find myself, it appears the message is to think of oneself above all else - let everyone else find their own way. How does a hurting person find their way?

One story in the Bible blesses me every time I read it. It's the story about a paralyzed man's friends. These four friends heard about Jesus healing the sick and decided they wanted to take their friend to Him. The four of them carried the paralyzed man. When they arrived at the home where Jesus was, they were unable to get him in because there were too many people in the way. I can just see these friends looking at the paralyzed man saying, 'Don't you worry, we'll get you there - to Him no matter what it takes.' They made a hole in the roof of the house and let the man down to be healed by Jesus. What great friends. We'll get you there- was the only thing they had on their minds. This scripture reference is found in the second chapter of the Gospel of Mark.

I have friends like that. My friend wanted to get me help so much she took me to a Bible study in the basement of the home of a man of God that prayed for me. My life was saved and changed. Do you have friends like that? Are you a friend like that?

Another of my favorite scripture references is in Nehemiah 4:14, which says, 'when Nehemiah saw *their fear*, he stood and said to everyone - "Do not be afraid ... confidently remember the Lord who is great and awesome, and with courage from Him fight for your brothers, your sons, your daughters, your wives, and for your homes." ' Fight for them. Fight for the ones you know - the ones struggling with addiction, depression, heartache, loneliness, eating disorders, and all other struggles. You may be the only one fighting for them - along with the Savior, of course.

Yes, I think we are our brothers' keepers. Also in the Bible, in Esther- 8.6, it tells us Esther saw her people were in danger and she expressed, "How can I bear to see disaster fall on my people? How can I bear to see the destruction of my family?"

Do you feel at a loss? Do our prayers work for others who are not praying for themselves? I say, "Yes." Prayer is the mystery of Christianity. We are commanded to pray. The Word of God assures us that, "the effectual, fervent prayer of a righteous man avails much." James 5.16. Also, we see in Daniel, chapter 9, that Daniel prayed for his country- a country NOT praying for itself. We can make a difference.

I do not know everyone and I don't know everyone's struggle, but my prayer is for you struggling one - is for hope and help, for you to know God and loved ones are with you and care and for others of you to hold the hand of everyone you know is struggling and walk with them, care for them, love them. For you to pray for them to be free of the struggles they face and find hope and healing. Don't worry about praying the perfect words. God wants this for them, so these prayers will be answered. His Will be done on Earth as it is in Heaven. Amen.

Write how you feel Jesus wants you to feel about others and how you do feel about them.

_____
_____
_____
_____
_____
_____
_____
_____
_____
_____
_____
_____
_____
_____
_____
_____
_____
_____
_____
_____
_____

# Day 24 - Looking for the Light

Many may ask- "How would a devotion about looking for the Light apply to me?" Maybe it wouldn't, maybe it would. I know I went looking for the Light until I found it to help me with some struggles.

There is an old saying, "It takes one to know one." I never understood that until I became one- a struggling person. For instance, I understood that no one knew and understood someone who struggled with alcohol or other addictions as one who experienced these struggles themselves. I think my talent is in identifying those struggling with deep hurts that they may not even know are inside.

Some say, 'leave the past in the past,' or 'just forget things and move on,' as well as other well - meaning words of advice. These may not be the most helpful suggestions though. Do deep hurts of the past just go away with time? I do not think I can be convinced of this.

Recently I met more people that convinced me that past hurts that are very deep do not just disappear with time, but shape our thoughts and actions and things that happen to us- in positive as well as negative ways. I find myself wanting to ask, "Were you loved properly?" "Were you protected?" "Can you say someone made you feel like you were the most special and loved little one in the whole world?" "Did anyone squeeze you in their arms to tell you how much you meant to them?" "Were there cruel words spoken to you by others that hurt deeply?"

When seeking truth and the Light, I remembered the nursery rhyme,

"Pussy cat, pussy cat,

where have you been?

I've been to England to see the Queen.

Pussy cat, pussy cat, what saw you there?

I saw a mouse run under her chair."

What I realized when I read this rhyme is that this cat was in the presence of greatness and royalty, however, only noticed an insignificant mouse run under the chair. It was illuminated to me that we, at times, disregard the 'real' or 'significant' issues, while we notice less significant 'mice' run under the chair. To clarify, issues with addiction, social isolation, compulsive behaviors, eating disorders, anxiety, and such, are all issues that need help, but they really signify deeper hurts inside the person struggling with these outward behaviors. These deep hurts go unnoticed and unaddressed because so much attention is paid to the symptom of the struggle instead of the reason for the struggle. And to clarify, I do not think struggles are 'insignificant.'

I am convinced all of us are 'bumped' in this fallen world. We all at times received a less than expected deal or treatment. Whether this was the loss of a parent or significant person in life, abuse of any kind, lack of guidance or affirmation as a child, school traumas, made to feel as if we do not measure up, as well as many other hurts that happen on a daily basis. These can be a cause of significant hurts that remain deep in our beings - especially if they happened when we were young.

I also realize there is a 'stigma' in admitting to others that we struggle. For goodness sake, there are medications to make us feel better when we really don't. We live in a world of Prozac and Xanax to solve all the problems we seem to face. I wanted real answers and solutions and not cover up medications to get me through the days.

That is why I sought the Light and sought answers in life. I felt misunderstood and abandoned, however, my search led me to the scriptures that helped me see Jesus as being there each step of my life each day. I was touched when I read that now and when I was a child in particular that in heaven my angels were always in the presence of and looked upon the Father Who is in heaven. (Matthew 8.10) I realized He was always connected to me personally and intimately.

Could there be deep hurts inside that have been there a long time? Do you think no one was there when you needed someone to be there? Do you think time has passed and things should no longer bother you, but something deep inside feels confused or sad or do things you don't understand or think less of yourself than you should?

Write your inner thoughts and struggles. Take them to Jesus for His care and help.

# Day 25 - **Tough Love**

Love is tough. I don't always know what to say to others, but I sure do see love everywhere I look. For instance, my girlfriend's son recently moved 1,000 miles and many States away. She is heartbroken, but she loves him and wants him to be happy. She is tough.

My other girlfriend travels over 80 miles each day to fight alongside the team of doctors, nurses, physical therapists, respiratory therapists and others to save her husband's life as he struggles to recover from a recent surgery. She is tired but sees the little improvements each day and continues to hope in the recovery of the one she has loved for many years.

Another girlfriend is helping her daughter with her addiction struggles and recent legal concerns. She has spent thousands of dollars for legal help and is working overtime to pay for the debts incurred. She drives her places to show her she is not alone in her struggle. They spend time doing crafts like making wreaths of autumn pine cones, laughing, having coffee, and sharing time together. She wants her daughter to know she is loved. She shared with me that she told her daughter her commitment to her began with her first breath and will end with my friend's last breath. Tough love.

My other friend visits a man in a wheelchair every day to share lonely and long hours with him. They talk about sky diving experiences they both shared as well as other things 'guys' talk about. An expression of love day after day when he could be doing other things.

I see love when folks move family members into their homes that have nowhere else to go. Sharing a life and living arrangements can be difficult - sometimes we consider this an invasion of privacy and life, but tough love does what is necessary. My Grandfather taught me that you take care of the ones you love. Love is grocery shopping, cooking, doing wash, and all the other acts of love that go unnoticed in a usual day for others that need a hand. Sometimes it is more difficult with more in a home and sometimes the ones in the home have medical concerns. Tough love keeps plugging along.

Love is sharing a meal with a homeless person. Taking time to be friends with the friendless people. It is not just a 5-minute event to share someone's life and help when needed.

I often hear others say- give them 'tough love.' Usually they mean let them figure it all out by themselves - let them alone in the struggle.

Sometimes that helps folks get to the end of their ropes. I cannot go to places like the beach when the ones I love need help and love. I just cannot.

The toughest love I have experienced is saying good-bye. When it comes time for someone we love to go Home, it can be the hardest thing we ever do, but that is loving them too. I watched my brother in pain and unable to breathe and finally watched him go Home to be in Paradise with the God I love. I feel weak at times, but I know love is tough and will get me through.

I will bet you know people who love when it is not easy. When they are the only people that that struggling person has to help - make a meal, provide a home, share time. We are in this together. We are not alone.

1 Corinthians 13 tells me Love is... kind.. love bears all things, believes all things, hopes all things... love never fails. I could be the greatest person in the world with many talents and give to the poor and sacrifice beyond human comprehension... but if I do not have love, I am nothing.... now there is faith, hope, and love, but the greatest of these is love...

Write how your love meter is doing.

_____
_____
_____
_____
_____
_____
_____

# Day 26 - How Cool

When teaching children, they were precious to me and I wanted them to know just how special and unique they were. So, in one class, we talked about all their particular 'favorite' things. We made posters. On the posters, we put their favorite color, their favorite TV show, their favorite game, their favorite desert, etc. – and we talked about their favorite song.

One of my little boys had a speech impediment. Usually, we just went with the flow and had no issues because he could show us what he wanted or needed, but when we asked what his favorite song was, he mumbled, 'blamyamabla' - some gibberish we could not understand. I looked at my assistant. She shrugged her shoulders. We asked several times- same gibberish. So, we waited. When the little boy's mother came, we told her we couldn't understand what his favorite song was. We asked again, he answered the same. She immediately said, 'Oh, that's I Heard It Through the Grapevine.' (A song the advertisers in California borrowed for advertising their raisons)

There was no way we would have ever been able to interpret that, but moms know the most amazing things. He certainly had a wonderful mother who loved him very much and could understand the un- understandable. Something I also attribute to God about all of us.

The little picture of the raisons in today's blog reminds me every day that there are majestic mountains, valleys, rivers, oceans, birds of all sorts, animals, reptiles, and all the living creatures on planet Earth, but only one and unique you.

Psalm 139 tells me:

'O Lord, you have searched me [thoroughly] and know me.

You know when I sit down and when I rise up [my entire life, everything I do];
You understand my thought from afar.
3
You scrutinize my path and my lying down,
And You are intimately acquainted with all my ways.
4
Even before there is a word on my tongue [still unspoken],
Behold, O Lord, You know it all.
5
You have enclosed me behind and before,
And [You have] placed Your hand upon me.
6
Such [infinite] knowledge is too wonderful for

me;
It is too high [above me], I cannot reach it......

For You formed my innermost parts;
You knit me [together] in my mother's womb.
14
I will give thanks *and* praise to You, for I am fearfully and wonderfully made;
Wonderful are Your works,
And my soul knows it very well......

How precious also are Your thoughts to me, O God!
How vast is the sum of them!
18
If I could count them, they would outnumber the sand.'
Ps. 139.1-6, 13-14, 17-18

    The God of the universe thinks of each one of us more times each day than there are sand particles on the beach! I remember how I felt when I first read this - like Someone really loved me. He loves each and every one of the one and only you too!

Write how you see Jesus sees you and the ones you Do you find Him in everything?

_____
_____
_____
_____
_____
_____
_____
_____
_____

# Day 27 – Friendship Because Life is Hard

My Aunt's name was Mildred. Some called her Millie. As children, we could not say Mildred or Millie, so we called her Aunt Moddy. She was young at heart and drove a red Mustang. She told fascinating stories of giving children free ice cream cones when she worked at an ice cream stand. We never knew if her stories were true, but we loved hearing them.

Aunt Moddy filled our lives with laughter and fun, but when she was older, she became sick with cancer. After treatment, she lost her hair and wore wigs. When I visited her in the nursing home where she went to live, she sat on the side of her hospital bed laughing and talking- telling stories - continuing to make everyone smile and laugh. Looking back, she was brave and as I watched her grow weaker and weaker, I remember thinking how sad life is at moments.

As children, life was simple. We went to school, did homework, played after school, made friends, watched TV, and dreamed of being older.

Older people had money and could go wherever they wanted, stay up late, and do all the things we dreamed of doing. We thought everything would be great when we were finally 'older.' The Beach Boys even sang a song, "Wouldn't it be nice if we were older..."

Since becoming *older*, I wish I could sit and have a chat with the adults from my childhood. I would tell them how distressed I am because they made life look so simple and uncomplicated. They never seemed strained or worried. Time just seemed to go by easily as they did the things adults do. Now I see it all differently.

Sometimes life is filled with love and laughter and hard work pays off and all is well with the world. Other times life is challenging with sorrow, loss, grief, and struggle. The longer I live, the more I have said good - bye to beloved family members and friends and pets. I have watched treasured friends falter into memory losses and struggle with health issues. Some close to me have struggled with addiction or sorrow and personal loss. As we are older, there are mortgages, car payments, bills, good and bad relationships, responsibilities - all can be challenging events in a day-to-day life.

Good friends and family are priceless to me because they help me muddle through the ups and downs of life. As I share with them, they share with me. It is comforting to know 'I am not alone.' We share many of the same struggles, the same difficulties, and the same happy and sad times as many of those around us. We are in this together.

Write how you feel Jesus has given you friends and made life easier.

_____
_____
_____
_____
_____
_____
_____
_____
_____
_____
_____
_____
_____
_____
_____
_____
_____
_____
_____
_____
_____
_____
_____

# Day 28 – Words

I have only known how to speak one language. Everyone knows language is made up of words and words have meaning whether you 'sound out' words or your hands create words.

My brother shared how he was once asked to prepare a speech on words. He said he considered this assignment difficult because he couldn't think of what to say. I thought about this and decided what speech I would have prepared. I would have said words are everything. I cannot imagine a world without them. Words convey love, encouragement, sympathy, hope, well wishing, congratulations, comfort, and trust - not only to humans, but animals as well. Words convey information as well as urgency sometimes. We are taught to 'choose our words wisely.' Not only the 'words' we say are meaningful, but how we say them is meaningful. On many occasions, I have called friends just to hear the sounds of words because it made me feel connected and comforted.

Much of my life revolves around animals, so I consider how words apply to these speechless creatures. When training horses, we use 'aides' to train and direct them. Aides include hands on the reins to communicate to the horse, legs on their sides- also to communicate, shifting weight sends messages, and sometimes an artificial aide-such as a crop or spurs is used.

An additional aide I rely on is my voice. Tone and words convey messages to horses as well as most animals. Horses are smart and able to learn words such as trot, canter, walk, and 'ho' for stop. This is apparent when instructors ask riders to command the horse, and, at the words of the instructor, the horse obeys before the rider executes the request. Some instructors change the words for basic commands to avoid this, but smart horses learn the new words as well.

One day, my pacer - Mattie - and I were jogging when she kicked up at a fly. When her leg came down, she straddled the shaft. 'Oh no," I thought. I asked her to stop on the track. I talked to her as she allowed me to remove her harness, free her from the cart, move her leg over the lowered shaft, put her harness back on, reattach the cart to the harness, and jump back onto the jog cart to continue jogging. She calmly obeyed even though other horses jogged by her. This is amazing trust because racing horses are often excited to race when around other horses. Mattie stood with me quietly and calmly as I talked to her and asked her to stand still. She knew my voice and we safely corrected a potentially disastrous situation.

Words. I make sure I use them to communicate to the pets in my life, but also to tell people I love and appreciate how much I do. I want them to hear the words I hold in my heart for them as well as show them every time I am able.

Ephesians 4.29 tells us – 'Let no foul or polluting language, nor evil word, nor unwholesome or worthless talk (ever) come out of your mouth, but only such (speech) as is good and beneficial to the spiritual progress of others, as is fitting to the need and the occasion, that it may be a blessing and give grace (God's favor) to those who hear it.'

Write how you use your words.

_____
_____
_____
_____
_____
_____
_____
_____
_____
_____
_____
_____
_____
_____
_____
_____
_____

# Day 29 - Coincidence?

Many years ago, I attended a Christmas concert my stepdaughter sang in. Before she came to the stage, the younger children sang their songs. One sweet little song was, "Must Be Santa." The first graders were darling as they sang, "Cap on head..." and put their little hands on their heads. Then they patted their chests as they sang, 'suit of red.' The little ones continued, "Special night, beard that's white," and, of course, rubbed their chins. Then they sang, "Must be Santa."

For years I remembered that little song and wanted the music. I contacted the school, but was unable to obtain any music. I searched the internet and many stores. One Saturday, while working in Sandusky, Ohio, I shopped at a small flea market. I was amazed! On one of the tables was a children's Christmas song book with "Must Be Santa" as one of the songs. I purchased it for the high price of 25 cents! I still have it. Some may say this was a coincidence, however, I believe nothing is a coincidence and it was

God's way of showing me He not only knows everything about the universe and the world. He knows every detail about us. He knew I was looking for this book. Proverbs 16.33 says, "[even the events that seem accidental are really ordered by Him]."

Not convinced? Well, I have read the Amplified version of the Bible for many years. My original Bible is so worn; it is in 17 sections. I thought it time to purchase a new one. I looked for a very long time - in Christian bookstores, on Amazon, anywhere I thought I could buy one. No luck. Then, one day, I was shopping at a thrift store about 15 minutes from my Ohio home and what did I see? An Amplified Bible in perfect condition. The thrift store had a policy to give the Bibles in the store for free. I was amazed by the God I love finding something as simple as a Bible for me.

Still not convinced? Well, I love yellow flowers. It came to my attention that there are yellow lilacs. I only knew of white and lavender - which I already have both of. Money was a little tight one year and I was unable to order any flowers or shrubs. I had previously ordered roses from a company that sent me a box I was not expecting. Inside were lovely yellow lilacs. I called the company and they said to keep the box when I offered to send it back. Coincidence? Not in my book.

If you still are not convinced - one night, I was on-call for horses. I had just lost a job and wanted pizza for dinner, but did not have the extra money to spend. I was called to a farm where a young horse was having stomach pain. I treated the horse, but the owners asked me to stay the night because the weather was snowy and they did not think I would be able to make it back if the foal needed me. I stayed, they treated me to dinner. When he brought in the pizza, he said, 'I was going to get chicken, but I decided to get this. I hope this is ok.' I said, 'Yes, very ok.' He had no idea, but I did. I whispered a thanks to the God I love.

I have at least 100 stories just like these. Vehicles I bought over the years, clothing I desired and needed, and many other 'things' God provided from His rich and unending supply.

The Bible tells us the very hairs on our head are numbered. (Matthew 10.30) God is in the details for sure. The Bible also tells us nothing is trivial to God. (Job 36.5) That means He knows everything about you and me, the secret things we have in our hearts are not only known to Him, but very important to Him too. I am convinced of this. This is another way He wants to show us how much He loves us.

Write how God has surprised you with your needs.

_____
_____
_____
_____
_____
_____
_____

# Day 30 - Super heroes

Many of us have a favorite Superhero whose super powers we admire - Superman with his ability to fly, super strength, and the ability to leap from tall buildings, Spiderman with his ability to scale tall buildings, swing from building to building, tie the bad guys up with his webs, or Batman in his bat-mobile fighting crime in Gotham city. What they have in common is they use their super powers for good.

In real life, I see superheroes all around. I met some of them in the halls of long term care facilities and patient rooms. I witnessed their superpowers of love and kindness as I spotted them fixing the ladies' hair, picking out favorite outfits, making sure the men were shaved, and doing every other little task to make these residents' lives nice. I saw them singing to patients, playing games, reading to some, sitting beside windows and talking for hours, and feeding others.

Other superheroes I have come to know are moms and dads of special needs children struggling with various physical conditions- from muscular dystrophy to paralysis to cerebral palsy and more. Parents and grandparents who care for these children day after day have always made me appreciate how love drives those in life to do what others may consider difficult or impossible. These heroes care for their little ones - taking them to frequent doctor or hospital visits, going through all the ups and downs of medical issues that arise, and kiss them and love them all day long.

Some superheroes care for aging parents or mates or injured family members day after day. One superhero came to my life as a friend. His wife later told me how he felt I was alone and he wanted them to 'take me under their wings.' They frequently invited me to dinner and walks in the park, made wooden jumping poles for my horses, shared every achievement with me, bought equipment they knew me and my horses would cherish, drove me and my injured horse to the veterinary clinic in Columbus, Ohio, and were there for me in many, many ways. Over the years I realized I never recognized the love I was shown specially by my friends. They were superheroes sent to make my life better.

Many make sacrifices and consider their care routine and just part of each day. I have come to realize that sometimes we do not change situations. Disability is still present; worsening medical conditions, addictions, struggles, etc., may remain, but we have the ability to use our superpowers of love and kindness and patience and hard work to ease the suffering and struggle of others.

One favorite story I love goes like this - a man was walking down the road and happened upon a robin lying on its back, with its feet in the air. "Little Robin, why are you lying on your back in the middle of the road?" the man asked. "The sky is falling, the sky is falling!" the Robin replied. "But why are your feet sticking up in the air?" the man pressed. "Because," said the little bird, "one must do what one can."

Write about a superhero you know. Are you a superhero to someone?

# Day 31 - **Resurrection Sunday**

Easter is the basis of Christianity. It means different things to each person. At times it has been fun hunting eggs and baskets of candy hidden intended to be found and enjoyed. I have enjoyed Easter bunnies and lambs and ham for dinner as well as new outfits and special shoes for church and family Easter celebration.

Over 40 years ago Easter came to mean something more to me. Sitting in my pew I saw the sun streaming in the window. It was if it were the first Resurrection Sunday ever. We sang:

"On a hill far away, stood an old rugged Cross
The emblem of suffering and shame
And I love that old Cross where
the Dearest and Best
For a world of lost sinners was slain"

I was a broken person, a sinner, in need - in need of a Savior. As I bowed my knees to give my heart and life to the God I love and would love forever, the Cross became more to me than I could ever imagine. They crucified Jesus thinking it was over and it was not. His death turned to life and His great reversal became my great reversal. It changed:

Death to life
Defeat to victory
Hate to love
Anxiety to peace
Loss to gain
Pain to healing
Sadness to happiness
Depression to release
Guilt to forgiveness
Bondage to freedom
Addiction to deliverance

    The Cross is everything to me. It is the symbol of where Jesus died and rose again so I could know Him and His love. He became my Father, my Friend, my Provider, Protector, Way Maker, Author and Finisher of my faith, the One Who sees me and knows all about me, Everything. I am not ashamed of the Cross and Gospel of Jesus Christ because it is the Power of God to salvation - to all answered prayers, deliverance, faith, enlightenment, forgiveness, overcoming, life, going to heaven for eternity- everything. (Romans 1.16)

    The words came to life to me that Resurrection Sunday so many years ago as we continued to sing:

"So I'll cherish the old rugged Cross
Till my trophies at last I lay down

I will cling to the old rugged Cross
And exchange it some day for a crown"

I reflect on the Words in the Bible - if anyone else is god - serve them, but as 'for me and my house, we will serve the Living God' - the Lord - the Resurrected One each and every Easter and each and every day. (Joshua 24.15)

Share what Easter means to you and how you remember the Cross each day.

_____
_____
_____
_____
_____
_____
_____
_____
_____
_____
_____
_____
_____
_____
_____
_____
_____
_____
_____
_____
_____
_____

# **Bonus Day - Broken Pieces**

One of my favorite things to do in Florida is walk the beaches searching for shells. I never realized shells have specific names- like turretella, yellow land snail, Florida welk, scallops, Telescopium, angel wings or concus aulicus- to name a few. I simply call them clam shells, conchs, spiral shells, and pretty ones. Once I found a sand dollar and a starfish. Friends enjoy showing me the shells they found. Of all the shells I find, the ones I treasure most are the broken ones. I find more fragments of shells than perfect, whole shells. I collect the fragments of shells to add to shell crafts because I think they are still beautiful.

The broken shells remind me of me - broken and imperfect. So many times I catch myself saying exactly what I did not want to say. I wish I had the opportunity to relive moments and do them better a second time around. Why did I become impatient? Why did I give someone the impression I had no time for them? Why did I need to feel superior to someone else? Regretting moments is an ongoing battle. New Year's Eve is approaching. I want to be better. I want those around me know how much I appreciate them, how kind and helpful they are to me, and how they make my life better just being in it. I want to choose words that let them know they are valuable and worthwhile.

Sometimes the broken shells remind me of people I love. It seems easier to accept imperfection in myself than those around me. I want them to know I see the beauty in them, the value in them. Throughout every New Year I want to be patient and kind. I want to believe the best in all around me and never notice if anyone does wrong to me. I want them to know they are special to me- every moment, every day. I want to be there to share their struggles as well as their celebrations.

A thanks- to those who have seen me at my best and at my worst and cannot tell the difference because they love me so much. I want to love everyone else the same.

Write if you feel broken at times. Write how you respond to others who are broken.

_____
_____
_____
_____
_____-
_____
_____
_____
_____

# Bonus Day - Devotion

I lived among the Amish for many years. Not only were they faithful friends to me, I saw devotion to their faith that inspires me. They take God seriously and in every way, respect, honor, and reverence Him. They do so in their talk, their way of life, and their worship. I think I am too casual sometimes.

I also see sincere and tender devotion to faith in Jewish people. While reading a book written by a Holocaust survivor, Elie Wiesel, called 'Night,' I was humbled and touched. He witnessed and experienced tremendous cruelty and watched the offenders kill his father. He was made to go hungry, worry, be afraid, walk naked in cold weather, have his tooth removed for gold without anesthesia, watch those around him be killed or burned or die from starvation or exhaustion and many other atrocities.

In His book he wrote, 'Some talked of God, of His mysterious ways... But I had ceased to pray. How I sympathized with Job! I did not deny God's existence, but I doubted His absolute justice." Wiesel goes on, "On the eve of Rosh

Hashanah, the last day of that accursed year, the whole camp was electric with the tension which was in all our hearts. In spite of everything, this day was different from any other. The last day of the year. The word 'last' rang very strangely. What if it were indeed the last day? They gave us our evening meal, a very thick soup, but no one touched it. We wanted to wait until after prayers. At the place of assembly, surrounded by the electrified barbed wire, thousands of silent Jews gathered, their faces stricken. Night was falling. Other prisoners continued to crowd in, from every block, able suddenly to conquer time and space and submit both to their will. **Ten thousand** men had come to attend the solemn service... 'Blessed be the Name of the Eternal!' Thousands of voices repeated the benediction, thousands of men prostrated themselves like trees before a tempest. 'Blessed be the Name of the Eternal!' I heard the voice of the officiant raised up, powerful yet at the same time broken, amid the tears, sobs, the sighs of the whole congregation: 'all the earth and the Universe are God's!' He kept stopping every moment, as though he did not have the strength to find meaning beneath the words. The melody choked in his throat."

Eli Weisel also goes on to say, "But these men here, whom (are suffering) ... They pray before You! They praise Your Name!' (and say) "All creation bears witness to the Greatness of God!" .... I stood amid that praying congregation, observing it like a stranger."

The image of starving, suffering, frightened men face down on the ground praising God in the midst of thousands of children being burned in pits, six crematories working night and day, on Sundays and feast days, Auschwitz, Birkenau, Buna, and so many factories of death, fathers, mothers, brothers ending in the crematory, tears at my heart.

I cast no stones at Eli Weisel. He lost faith temporarily in the midst of the horror. I have never known hunger or torture. My life has been blessed in a way I cannot comprehend what these men and women went through or what others have suffered even today. I go to my knees to ask the God of the Universe to forgive my unappreciative heart and help me to always Praise the Eternal One no matter my circumstance. If they could praise Him in the horrific circumstance they endured, I could in my circumstances as well. I want to be sincere in my devotion to the God of the Universe no matter what.

Write your thoughts about your devotion to God.

_____
_____
_____
_____
_____
_____
_____
_____
_____

www.ingramcontent.com/pod-product-compliance
Lightning Source LLC
Chambersburg PA
CBHW041957080526
**44588CB00021B/2779**